Let's Measure It!

The fish in the bowl is one inch long.

What else is one inch?
Let's measure.

4 **The fish in the pail is two inches long.**

What else is two inches?
Let's measure.

Do not feed the fish.

The fish in the aquarium is three inches long.

feather

cherry

mushroom

duckling

What else is three inches?
Let's measure.

8 The fish in the river is four inches long.

What else is four inches?
Let's measure.

9

The fish in the lake is five inches long.

Camping Supplies

flashlight

cooking pot

Band Aides

sleeping bag

tent

What else is five inches?

The fish in the ocean is six inches long.

What else is six inches?

Let's measure everything!

feather

Can you measure a friend?